RUNNI
POEMS FO

Running lightly ...

Poems for Young People

Selected and Edited by
Tom Mullins

MERCIER PRESS
PO Box 5, 5 French Church Street, Cork
and
16 Hume Street, Dublin

Trade enquiries to CMD DISTRIBUTION,
55a Spruce Avenue, Stillorgan Industrial Park, Blackrock, Dublin

ISBN 1 85635 193 9

10 9 8 7 6 5 4 3 2 1

A CIP record for this book is available from the British Library.

Printed in Ireland by Colour Books Ltd.

Contents

For

Juliet, Ruth, Elizabeth, Jane and Andrew

FOREWORD

MOST PEOPLE SEEM TO USE POETRY for special events, such as celebrating success, falling in love or honouring the dead; but poetry should not be just kept for such events.

I learned this from a teacher, Charles Keane, who taught me in primary school. He was a remarkable person. While teaching any subject, maths or history or religion, he was likely to say a poem or break into song ... perhaps it was his way of keeping sane while teaching! Whatever the reason Charles showed that poetry and song were as necessary to him as eating and breathing; they were essential ingredients of his everyday life. He took great pleasure in just saying the poems and singing the songs and he delighted in sharing them with others.

This selection was chosen with those two pleasure principles of savouring the words and sharing the experience as guides.

The poems and songs are best said aloud so that we actually hear the rhythms and sounds of the words and feel their shape and texture in our mouths ... much of the pleasure of poetry comes from this. Another pleasure in poetry is seeing some feelings and ideas we have had ourselves put into words that seem just right and memorable. 'What oft was thought, but ne'er so well expressed'. It is for this reason, in the main, that the book is organised under separate sections with such titles as *Safe and Warm, Out on the Edge, Moments* and so on.

Finally, poetry can surprise by showing a new way of seeing something, by perhaps making the ordinary seem extraordinary. This happens unpredictably and varies from poem to poem and from person to person. But in coming to read poetry the surest way of destroying the pleasure it brings is to look for hidden meanings. Charles Keane, I suspect, never looked for them and yet poetry sustained him throughout his life.

Elizabeth Bishop, an American poet, one said 'that poems were like imaginary gardens with real toads in them'. The best way into poetry is to enjoy and explore every aspects of the imaginary garden and forget about the toads ... they will appear in their own good time ... trust them.

TOM MULLINS
OCTOBER, 1997

Safe and Warm

Early in the Morning

Early in the morning
The water hits the rocks,
The birds are making noises
Like old alarum clocks,
The soldier on the skyline
Fires a golden gun
And over the back of the chimney-stack
Explodes the silent sun.

Charles Causley

Summer and Winter

When a warm dawn brings
the sun to your eyes,
blink three times –
it's time to rise.

When cold winds whistle
around your head,
pull it under the blankets
and stay in bed.

Michael Dugan

I Wish I Were a Wood-Louse

I wish I were a wood-louse,
In a green, mossy house,
Under a big flat stone:
I would roll into a ball
When people came to call,
And then they would leave me alone.

Anon.

The Window

Behind the blind I sit and watch
The people passing – passing by;
And not a single one can see
My tiny watching eye.

They cannot see my little room,
All yellowed with the shaded sun,
They do not even know I'm here;
Nor'll guess when I am gone.

Walter De La Mare

Brigid

Brigid, bring the cows
From the water shore
Now the sun is falling
Underneath the moor.

Bring them by the field-oak,
Bring them by the stone
That stands at the cross-way
With Bible pictures on.

In her hand she carries
A wand of green bay
As she brings the swaying herd
Slowly on its way.

The wild duck from their swimming,
The wild duck as they fly
Come at her calling
As she passes by.

Brigid, bring the cows
From the long shore,
Bring the milk and butter
To the hungry poor.

Charles Causley

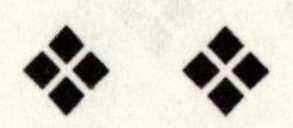

The Wood of Dromagh

Walking in the wood of Dromagh
I heard a chaffinch sing;
There were tears on the sun's eyelashes
and trees were spidering spring.

Standing in the wood of Dromagh
I heard a schoolboy call;
There was a treeroot throne on a twig red carpet
and wind waved fans over all.

Sitting in the wood of Dromagh
I heard the bluebells ring;
There were mauve primroses like mauve princesses
and saplings curtsying.

Dreaming in the wood of Dromagh
I heard a children's choir;
There was no falling bud in all the wooded world
and no more slashing ire.

Jerome Kiely

Tall Nettles

Tall nettles cover up, as they have done
These many springs, the rusty harrow, the plough
Long worn out, and the roller made of stone:
Only the elm butt tops the nettles now.

This corner of the farmyard I like most:
As well as any bloom upon a flower
I like the dust on the nettles, never lost
Except to prove the sweetness of a shower.

EDWARD THOMAS

After the Rains

After the rains,
when I opened my door
the spiders were at it
as hard as before,

mending their nets,
as the sun came again,
the patient, dependable
fly-fishermen.

N. M. BODECKER

Out on the Edge

RUNNING LIGHTLY ...

Running lightly over spongy ground,
Past the pasture of flat stones,
The three elms,
The sheep strewn on a field,
Over a rickety bridge
Toward the quick-water, wrinkling and rippling.

Hunting along the river,
Down among the rubbish, the bug-riddled foliage,
By the muddy pond-edge, by the bog-holes,
By the shrunken lake, hunting, in the heat of
 summer.

The shape of a rat?
 It's bigger than that.
 It's less than a leg
 And more than a nose,
 Just under the water
 It usually goes.

 Is it soft like a mouse?
 Can it wrinkle its nose?
 Could it come in the house
 On the tips of its toes?

 Take the skin of a cat
 And the back of an eel,
 Then roll them in grease –
 That's the way it would feel.

It's sleek as an otter
With wide webby toes
Just under the water
It usually goes.

THEODORE ROETHKE

OUT IN THE DARK

Out in the dark over the snow
The fallow fawns invisible go
With the fallow doe;
And the winds blow
Fast as the stars are slow.

Stealthily the dark haunts round
And, when the lamp goes, without sound
At a swifter bound
Than the swiftest hound,
Arrives, and all else is drowned;

And star and I and wind and deer
Are in the dark together – near,
Yet far – and fear
Drums on my ear
In that sage company drear.

How weak and little is the light,
All the universe of sight,
Love and delight,
Before the might,
If you love it not, of night.

EDWARD THOMAS

NOTHING

He thought he heard
A footstep on the stair,
'It's nothing,' he said to himself,
'Nothing is there.'
He thought then he heard
A snuffling in the hall,
'It's nothing,' he said again,
'Nothing at all.'
But he didn't open the door
In case he found nothing
Standing there,
On foot or tentacle or paw.
Timidly quiet he kept to his seat
While nothing stalked the house
On great big feet.
It was strange though

And he'd noticed this
When on his own before,
Nothing stalked throughout the house
But never through his door.
The answer he thought,
Was very plain. It was because there was
nothing there –
Again!

JULIE HOLDER

IN THE ORCHARD

There was a giant by the Orchard Wall
Peeping about on this side and on that,
And feeling in the trees. He was as tall
As the big apple tree, and twice as fat:
His beard poked out, all bristly-black, and there
Were leaves and gorse and heather in his hair.

He held a blackthorn club in his right hand,
And plunged the other into every tree,
Searching for something – You could stand
Beside him and not reach up to his knee,
So big he was – I trembled lest he should
Come trampling, round-eyed, down to where I stood.

I tried to get away – But, as I slid
Under a bush, he saw me, and he bent
Down deep at me, and said, *'Where is she hid?'*
I pointed over there, and off he went –

But, while he searched, I turned and simply flew
Round by the lilac bushes back to you.

JAMES STEPHENS

SOME ONE

Some one came knocking
At my wee, small door;
Some one came knocking,
I'm sure – sure – sure;
I listened, I opened,
I looked to left and right,
But naught there was a-stirring
In the still dark night;
Only the busy beetle
Tap-tapping in the wall,
Only from the forest
The screech-owl's call,
Only the cricket whistling
While the dewdrops fall,

So I know not who came knocking,
At all, at all, at all.

WALTER DE LA MARE

THE LURKERS

On our Estate
When it's getting late
In the middle of the night
They come in flocks
From beneath tower blocks
And crawl towards the light

Down the Crescent
Up the Drive
Late at night
They come alive
Lurking here and lurking there
Sniffing at the midnight air

Up the Shopping Centre
You might just hear their call
Something like a bin-bag
Moving by the wall

Lurking at the bus-stop
Seen through broken glass
Something dark and slimy
Down the underpass

On our Estate
When it's getting late
In the middle of the night
There are things that lurk
About their work
Till dawn puts them to flight.

ADRIAN HENRI

HOW MANY MILES TO BABYLON?

How many miles to Babylon?
Threescore and ten, Sir.

Can I get there by candlelight?
Oh yes, and back again, Sir.

If your heels are nimble and light,
You may get there by candlelight.

TRADITIONAL

The Door

A white door in a hawthorn hedge –
Who lives through there?
A sorcerer? A wicked witch
With serpents in her hair?

A king enchanted into stone?
A lost princess?
A servant girl who works all night
Spinning a cobweb dress?

A queen with slippers made of ice?
I'd love to see.
A white door in a hawthorn hedge–
I wish I had a key.

Richard Edwards

Dream Poem

I have not seen this house before
Yet room for room I know it well:
A thudding clock upon the stair,
A mirror slanted on the wall.

A round-pane giving on the park.
Above the hearth a painted scene
Of winter huntsmen and the pack.
A table set with fruit and wine.

Here is a childhood book, long lost.
I turn its wasted pages through:
Every word I read shut fast
In a far tongue I do not know.

Out of a thinness in the air
I hear the turning of a key
And once again I turn to see
The one who will be standing there.

CHARLES CAUSLEY

HAWTHORN WHITE

Hawthorn white, hawthorn red
Hanging in the garden at my head
Tell me simple, tell me true
When comes the winter what must I do?

I have a house with chimneys four
I have a silver bell on the door,
A single hearth and a single bed.

Not enough, the hawthorn said.

I have a lute, I have a lyre
I have a yellow cat by my fire,
A nightingale to my tree is tied.
That bird looks sick, the hawthorn sighed.

I write on paper pure as milk
I lie on sheets of Shantung silk,
On my green breast no sin has snowed.
You'll catch your death, the hawthorn crowed.

My purse is packed with a five-pound note
The watchdogs in my garden gloat.
I blow the bagpipe down my side.
Better blow your safe, the hawthorn cried.

My pulse is steady as my clock
My wits are wise as the weathercock.
Twice a year we are overhauled.
It's Double Summer-Time! the hawthorn called.

I have a horse with wings for feet
I have chicken each day to eat.
When I was born the church-bells rang.
Only one at a time, the hawthorn sang.

I have a cellar, I have a spread
The bronze blood runs round my bulkhead.
Why is my heart as light as lead?
Love is not there, the hawthorn said.

CHARLES CAUSLEY

If All the World were Paper

If all the world were paper,
  And all the sea were ink,
And all the trees were bread and cheese,
  How should we do for drink?

If all the world were sand-o
  Oh, then what should we lack-o?
If, as they say, there were no clay,
  How should we take tobacco?

If all our vessels ran-a,
  If none but had a crack-a;
If Spanish apes ate all the grapes,
  How should we do for sack-a?

If friars had no bald pates,
  Nor nuns had no dark cloisters;
If all the seas were beans and peas,
  How should we do for oysters?

If there had been no projects,
  Nor none that did great wrongs;
If fiddlers shall turn players all,
  How should we do for songs?

If all things were eternal,
  And nothing their end bringing;
If this should be, then how should we
  Here make an end of singing?

Anonymous

QUESTIONS AND ANSWERS

Where do you think that treasure lies?
Beyond the dark of the deepest skies.

How do I get there, by sky or by sea?
That's a question you shouldn't ask me.

The people there could be friend or foe?
Whatever you do will make them so.

When I arrive there, what shall I do?
Wait for the wise ones to visit you.

I'm fearful of going to a land so away?
The choice is yours, you can always stay.

No, I'm certain I'll go, from where do I start?
To find the direction look into your heart.

GABRIEL THOMAS

THROUGH OTHER EYES

Puddin' Song

Oh, who would be a puddin',
A puddin' in a pot,
A puddin' which is stood on
A fire which is hot?
O sad indeed the lot
Of puddin's in a pot.

I wouldn't be a puddin'
If I could be a bird,
If I could be a wooden
Doll, I wouldn't say a word.
Yes, I have often heard
It's grand to be a bird.

But as I am a puddin',
A puddin' in a pot,
I hope you get the stomachache
For eatin' me a lot.
I hope you get it hot,
You puddin'-eat' lot!

Norman Lindsay

My mother saw a dancing bear

My mother saw a dancing bear
By the schoolyard, a day in June.
The keeper stood with chain and bar
And whistle-pipe, and played a tune.

And bruin lifted up its head
And lifted up its dusty feet,
And all the children laughed to see
It caper in the summer heat.

They watched as for the Queen it died.
They watched it march. They watched it halt.
They heard the keeper as he cried,
'Now, roly-poly!' 'Somersault!'

And then, my mother said, there came
The keeper with a begging-cup,
The bear with burning coat of fur,
Shaming the laughter to a stop.

They paid a penny for the dance,
But what they saw was not the show;
Only, in bruin's aching eyes,
Far-distant forests, and the snow.

Charles Causley

Tom Bone

My name is Tom Bone,
I live all alone
In a deep house on Winter Street.
  Through my mud wall
  The wolf-spiders crawl
  And the mole has his beat.

On my roof of green grass
All the day footsteps pass
In the heat and the cold,
  As snug in a bed
  With my name at its head
  One great secret I hold.

Tom Bone, when the owls rise
In the drifting night skies
Do you walk round about?
  All the solemn hours through
  I lie down just like you
  And sleep the night out.

Tom Bone, as you lie there
On your pillow of hair,
What grave thoughts do you keep?
  Tom says, 'Nonsense and stuff!
  You'll know soon enough.
  Sleep, darling, sleep.'

Charles Causley

Monster

I saw a monster in the woods
As I was cycling by,
His footsteps smouldered in the leaves,
His breath made bushes die.

And when he raised his hairy arm
It blotted out the sun;
He snatched a pigeon from the sky
And swallowed it in one.

His mouth was like a dripping cave,
His eyes like pools of lead,
And when he growled I rode back home
And rushed upstairs to bed.

But that was yesterday and though
It gave me quite a fright,
I'm older now and braver so
I'm going back tonight.

I'll tie him up when he's asleep
And take him to the zoo.
The trouble is he's rather big ...
Will you come too?

Richard Edwards

SEAHORSE

O under the ocean waves
I gallop the seaweed lanes,
I jump the coral reef,
And all with no saddle or reins.

I haven't a flowing mane,
I've only this horsey face,
But under the ocean waves
I'm king of the steeplechase.

BLAKE MORRISON

HER BLINDNESS

In her blindness
the house became
a tapestry of touch.

The jagged end of a dresser
became a signpost
to the back-door,

bread crumbs crunching
under her feet told
her when to sweep

the kitchen floor;

the powdery touch
of dry leaves in
the flower-trough
said that geraniums
needed water.

I remember her beside
the huge December fire,
holding a heavy mug,
changing its position
on her lap; filling

the dark space
between her fingers
with the light
of bright memory.

THOMAS MCCARTHY

A Piper

A piper in the street today
Set up, and tuned, and started to play,
And away, away, away on the tide
Of his music we started; on every side
Doors and windows were opened wide,
And men left down their work and came,
And women with petticoats coloured like flame
And little bare feet that were blue with cold,
Went dancing back to the age of gold,
And all the world went gay, went gay,
For half an hour in the street today

Seumas O'Sullivan

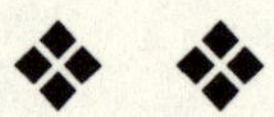

I'm Nobody! Who are You?

I'm Nobody! Who are you?
Are you – Nobody – Too?
Then there's a pair of us!
Don't tell! They'd banish us you know!

How dreary – to be – Somebody!
How public – like a Frog –
To tell your name – the livelong June –
To an admiring Bog!

Emily Dickinson

SONGS TO SING

I Know My Love

I know my love, by her way of walking
And I know my love, by her way of talking
And I know my love by her suit of blue,
But if my love leaves me, what would I do?
And yet she cries: 'I love you the best.'
But a troubled mind, sure can know no rest
And yet she cries: 'Bonny boys are few.'
But if my love loves me, what would I do?

There is a dance-hall at Mollakide
Where my true love goes every night
And there she sits on some strange lad's knee.
Well, don't you know now, that vexes me
And yet she cries, 'I love you the best,'
But a troubled mind, sure can know no rest.
And yet she cries, 'Bonny boys are few,'
But if my love leaves me, what would I do?

Anon.

Barbara Allen

In Scarlet town, where I was born,
There was a fair maid dwellin'
Made ev'ry youth cry well-a-day,
Her name was Barbara Allen.

'Twas in the merry month of May
The green buds they were swellin'
Sweet William on his death-bed lay
For the sake of Bar'bra Allen.

He sent his servant to her house
The place where she was dwellin'
Said, 'You must come to my master's house,
If your name be Bar'bra Allen.'

A dying man, O look at me
One kiss from you will cure me
One kiss from me, you shall never get
While your poor heart is breaking.

As she was walking down the fields
She heard some birds a-singing
And as they sang, they seemed to say,
'Hard-hearted Bar'bra Allen.'

Come Mother, come, make up my bed
Make it both long and narrow
My true love died for me yesterday
I'll die for him tomorrow.

And he was buried in Edmundstone
And she was buried in Cold Harbour
And out of him grew roses red
And out of her green brier.

They grew and grew so very high
Till they could grow no higher
And at the top grew a true lover's knot
And around it twined green brier.

ANON.

I BOUGHT ME A CAT

I bought me a cat, my cat pleased me
I fed my cat under yonder tree
My cat says 'Fiddle eye fee'.

I bought me a duck, my duck pleased me
I fed my duck under yonder tree
My duck says 'Quaa, quaa'
My cat says 'Fiddle eye fee'.

I bought me a goose, my goose pleased me
I fed my goose under yonder tree
My goose says 'Quaw, quaw'
My duck says 'Quaa, quaa'

My cat says 'Fiddle eye fee'.

I bought me a hen, my hen pleased me
I fed my hen under yonder tree
My hen says 'Shimmy shack, shimmy shack'
My goose says 'Quaw, quaw'
My duck says 'Quaa, quaa'
My cat says 'fiddle eye fee'.

I bought me a pig, my pig pleased me
I fed my pig under younder tree
My pig says 'Griffey, griffey'
My hen says 'Shimmy shack, shimmy shack'
My goose says 'Quaw, quaw'
My duck says 'Quaa, quaa'
My cat says 'Fiddle eye fee'.

I bought me a cow, my cow pleased me
I fed my cow under yonder tree
My cow says 'Baw, baw'
My pig says 'Griffey, griffey'
My hen says 'Shimmy shack, shimmy shack'
My goose says 'Quaw, quaw'
My duck says 'Quaa, quaa'
My cat says 'Fiddle eye fee'.

I bought me a horse, my horse pleased me
I fed my horse under yonder tree
My horse says 'Neigh, neigh'
My cow says 'Baw, baw'
My pig says 'Griffey, griffey'

My hen says 'Shimmy shack, shimmy shack'
My goose says 'Quaw, quaw'
My duck says 'Quaa, quaa'
My cat says 'Fiddle eye fee'.

I bought me a wife, my wife pleased me
I fed my wife under yonder tree
My wife says 'Honey, honey'
My horse says 'Neigh, neigh'
My cow says 'Baw, baw'
My pig says 'Griffey, griffey'
My hen says 'Shimmy shack, shimmy shack'
My goose says 'Quaw, quaw'
My duck says 'Quaa, quaa'
My cat says 'Fiddle eye fee'.

TRADITIONAL

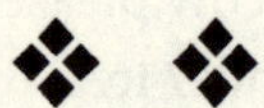

THERE WAS AN OLD WOMAN

There was an old woman who swallowed a fly;
I wonder why
She swallowed a fly.
Poor old woman, she's sure to die.

There was an old woman who swallowed a spider;
That wriggled and jiggled and wriggled inside her;

She swallowed the spider to catch the fly,
I wonder why
She swallowed a fly.
Poor old woman, she's sure to die.

There was an old woman who swallowed a bird;
How absurd
To swallow a bird.
She swallowed the bird to catch the spider,
That wriggled and jiggled and wriggled inside her.
She swallowed the spider to catch the fly,
I wonder why
She swallowed a fly
Poor old woman, she's sure to die.

There was an old woman who swallowed a cat;
Fancy that!
She swallowed a cat;
She swallowed the cat to catch the bird
She swallowed the bird to catch the spider,
That wriggled and jiggled and wriggled insider her.
She swallowed the spider to catch the fly,
I wonder why
She swallowed a fly.
Poor old woman, she's sure to die.

There was an old woman who swallowed a dog;
She went the whole hog
And swallowed a dog;
She swallowed the dog to catch the cat,
She swallowed the cat to catch the bird,

She swallowed the bird to catch the spider,
That wriggled and jiggled and wriggled inside her.
She swallowed the spider to catch the fly,
I wonder why
She swallowed a fly.
Poor old woman, she's sure to die.

There was an old woman who swallowed a cow;
I wonder how
She swallowed a cow;
She swallowed the cow to catch the dog,
She swallowed the dog to catch the cat,
She swallowed the cat to catch the bird,
She swallowed the bird to catch the spider,
That wriggled and jiggled and wriggled inside her.
She swallowed the spider to catch the fly,
I wonder why
She swallowed a fly.
Poor old woman, she's sure to die.

There was an old woman who swallowed a horse;
She died of course!

TRADITIONAL

Yankee Doodle

Yankee Doodle went to town,
He rode a little pony,
He stuck a feather in his hat
And called it macaroni.

Yankee Doodle fa, so, la,
Yankee Doodle dandy.
Yankee Doodle fa, so la,
Buttermilk and brandy.

Yankee Doodle went to town
To buy a pair of trousers,
He swore he could not see the town
For so many houses.

Yankee Doodle fa, so, la,
Yankee Doodle dandy.
Yankee Doodle fa, so, la,
Buttermilk and brandy.

Traditional

She Moved Through the Fair

My young love said to me, 'My brothers won't mind,
And my parents won't slight you for your lack of kind.'
Then she stepped away from me, and this she did say
'It will not be long, love, till our wedding day.'

She stepped away from me and she moved through the
    fair,
And fondly I watched her go here and go there,
Then she went her way homeward with one star awake
As the swan in the evening moves over the lake.

The people were saying no two were e'er wed
But one had a sorrow that never was said,
And I smiled as she passed with her goods and her gear
And that was the last that I saw of my dear.

I dreamt it last night that my young love came in,
So softly she entered, her feet made no din;
She came close beside me, and this she did say
'It will not be long, love, till our wedding day.'

Padraic Colum

I'll Tell My Ma

I'll tell my ma when I go home,
The boys won't leave the girls alone,
They pull my hair, they stole my comb,
But that's all right 'till I go home.
She is handsome, she is pretty,
She is the belle of Belfast City,
She is courtin' one, two, three,
Please won't you tell me who is she?

Albert Mooney says he loves her,
All the boys are fighting for her,
They rap at the door, and they ring the bell,
Saying O my true love are you well?
Out she comes as white as snow,
Rings on her fingers, bells on her toes,
Old Johnny Murray says she'll die,
If she doesn't get the fellow with the roving eye.

Anon.

A Fox Jumped Up

A fox jumped up one winter's night,
And begged the moon to give him light,
For he'd many miles to trot that night
Before he reached his den O!
  Den O! Den O!
For he'd many miles to trot that night
Before he reached his den O!

The first place he came to was farmer's yard,
Where the ducks and the geese declared it hard
That their nerves should be shaken and their rest so
  marred
By a visit from Mr Fox O!
    Fox O! Fox O!
That their nerves should be shaken and their rest so
  marred
By a visit from Mr Fox O!

He took the grey goose by the neck,
And swung him right across his back;
The grey goose cried out, Quack, quack, quack,
With his legs hanging dangling down O!
    Down O! Down O!
They grey goose cried out, Quack, quack, quack,
With his legs hanging dangling down O!

Old Mother Slipper Slopper jumped out of bed,
And out of the window she popped her head:
Oh! John John, John, they grey goose is gone,

And the fox is off to his den O!
    Den O! Den O!
Oh! John, John, John, the grey goose is gone,
And the fox is off to his den O!

John ran up to the top of the hill,
And blew his whistle loud and shrill;
Said the fox, That is very pretty music; still –
I'd rather be in my den O!
    Den O! Den O!
Said the fox, That is very pretty music; still –
I'd rather be in my den O!

The fox went back to his hungry den,
And his dear little foxes, eight, nine, ten;
Quoth they, Good Daddy, you must go there again,
If you bring such cheer from the farm O!
    Farm O! Farm O!
Quoth they, Good Daddy, you must go there again,
If you bring such cheer from the farm O!

The fox and his wife, without any strife,
Said they never ate a better goose in all their life:
They did very well without fork or knife,
And the little ones picked the bones O!
    Bones O! Bones O!
They did very well without fork or knife,
And the little ones picked the bones O!

ANON.

My Aunt Jane

My Aunt Jane, she took me in,
She gave me tea out of her wee tin,
Half a bap with sugar on the top,
Three black lumps out of her wee shop.
Half a bap with sugar on the top,
Three black lumps out of her wee shop.

My Aunt Jane has a bell at the door,
A white stone step and a clean swept floor,
Candy apples and hard green pears,
Conversation lozenges.
Candy apples and hard green pears,
Conversation lozenges.

My Aunt Jane, she's so smart,
She bakes wee rings in an apple tart,
And when Hallowe'en comes round,
Fornenst that tart I'm always found.
And when Hallowe'en comes round,
Fornenst that tart I'm always found.

My Aunt Jane has a great wee shop,
Lucky bags and lime juice rock,
Cinnamon lumps and yellow man,
And big brandy balls in a bright tin can.
Cinnamon lumps and yellow man,
And big brandy balls in a bright tin can.

My Aunt Jane, she took me in,

She gave me tea out of her wee tin,
Half a bap with sugar on the top,
Three black lumps out of her wee shop.
Half a bap with sugar on the top,
Three black lumps out of her wee shop.

TRADITIONAL

BRENNAN ON THE MOOR

It's of a fearless highwayman a story now I'll tell:
His name was Willie Brennan, and in Ireland he did dwell;
'Twas on the Limerick mountains he commenced his wild
career,
Where many a wealthy gentleman before him shook with
fear.

Brennan on the moor, Brennan on the moor,
Bold and yet undaunted stood young Brennan on the moor.

A brace of loaded pistols he carried night and day,
He never robb'd a poor man upon the king's highway;
But what he'd taken from the rich, like Turpin and Black
Bess,
He always did divide it with the widow in distress.

One night he robbed a packman, his name was [Pedlar]

Bawn;
They travelled on together, till day began to dawn;
The pedlar seeing his money gone, likewise his watch and chain,
He at once encountered Brennan and robbed him back again.

When Brennan saw the pedlar was as good a man as he,
He took him on the highway, his companion for to be;
The pedlar threw away his pack without any more delay,
And proved a faithful comrade until his dying day.

One day upon the highway Willie he sat down,
He met the Mayor of Cashel, a mile outside the town,
The Mayor he knew his features, 'I think, young man,' said he,
'Your name is Willie Brennan, you must come along with me.'

As Brennan's wife had gone to town provisions for to buy,
When she saw her Willie, she began to weep and cry;
He says, 'Give me that tenpence'; as soon as Willie spoke,
She handed him the blunderbuss from underneath her cloak.

Then with his loaded blunderbuss, the truth I will unfold,
He made the Mayor to tremble, and robbed him of his gold;
One hundred pounds was offered for his apprehension there,
And with his horse and saddle to the mountains did

repair.

Then Brennan being an outlaw upon the mountain high,
Where cavalry and infantry to take him they did try,
He laughed at them with scorn, until at length, it's said,
By a false-hearted young man he was basely betrayed.

In the County of Tipperary, in a place they called Clonmore,
Willie Brennan and his comrade that day did suffer sore;
He lay among the fern which was thick upon the field,
And nine wounds he had received before that he did yield.

Then Brennan and his companion knowing they were betrayed,
He with the mounted cavalry a noble battle made;
He lost his foremost finger, which was shot off by a ball;
So Brennan and his comrade they were taken after all.

So they were taken prisoners, in irons they were bound,
And conveyed to Clonmel jail, strong walls did them surround;
They were tried and found guilty, the judge made this reply,
'For robbing on the king's highway you are both condemned to die.'

Farewell unto my wife, and to my children three,
Likewise my aged father, he may shed tears for me,
And to my loving mother, who tore her grey locks and

cried,
Saying, 'I wish, Willie Brennan, in your cradle you had died.'

ANON.

I GAVE MY LOVE

I gave my love a cherry without a stone;
I gave my love a chicken without a bone;
I gave my love a ring without an end;
I gave my love a baby with no crying.

How can there be a cherry without a stone?
How can there be a chicken without a bone?
How can there be a ring without an end?
How can there be a baby with no crying?

A cherry, when it's blooming, it has no stone;
A chicken, when it's pipping, it has no bone;
A ring, when it's rolling, it has no end;
A baby, when it's sleeping, has no crying

ANON.

Casey Jones

Casey Jones was engineer,
Told his fireman not to fear.
All he wanted was a boiler hot,
Run in Canton 'bout four o'clock.

One Sunday mornin' it was drizzlin' rain,
Looked down road an' saw a train.
Fireman says: 'Let's make a jump;
Two locomotives an' dey bound to bump.'

Casey Jones, I know him well,
Told de fireman to ring de bell.
Fireman jump an' say 'Goodbye,
Casey Jones, you're bound to die.'

Went on down to de depot track,
Beggin' my honey to take me back,
She turn 'roun' some two or three times:
'Take you back when you learn to grind.'

Women in Kansas, all dressed in red,
Got de news dat Casey was dead.
De womens in Jackson, all dressed in black,
Said, in fact, he was a cracker-jack.

Anon.

The Butcher Boy

In London town where I did dwell,
A butcher boy I loved him well,
He courted me for many a day;
He stole from me my heart away.

There is an inn in that same town,
And there my love he sits him down;
He takes a strange girl on his knee
And tells her what he wouldn't tell me.

The reason is, I'll tell you why,
Because she's got more gold than I.
But gold will melt and silver fly,
And in time of need be as poor as I.

I'll go upstairs and make my bed.
'There is nothing to do,' my mother said.
My mother she has followed me,
Saying, 'What is the matter, my daughter dear?'

'O mother dear, you little know
What pains or sorrow or what woe!
Go get a chair and sit me down,
With pen and ink I'll write all down.'

She wrote a letter, she wrote a song,
She wrote a letter, she wrote it long;
On every line she dropped a tear,
At every verse cried, 'Willy dear!'

Her father he came home that night
Enquiring for his heart's delight;
He went upstairs, the door he broke,
He found her hanging on a rope.

He took a knife and cut her down,
And in her bosom these lines he found:
'O what a foolish girl was I
To hang myself for a butcher's boy.

'Go dig my grave both wide and deep,
Put a marble stone at my head and feet,
And on my grave place a turtle dove
To show the world that I died for love.'

ANON.

MY MOTHER SAID

My mother said that I never should
Play with the gypsies in the wood,
The wood was dark; the grass was green;
In came Sally with a tambourine.

I went to the sea – no ship to get across;
I paid ten shillings for a blind white horse;

I up on his back and was off in a crack,
Sally tell my Mother I shall never come back.

ANON.

'I KNOW WHERE I'M GOING'

I know where I'm going,
And I know who's going with me.
I know who I love,
But the dear knows who I'll marry.

I'll have stockings of silk,
Shoes of fine green leather,
Combs to buckle my hair
And a ring for every finger.

Feather beds are soft,
Painted rooms are bonny:
But I'd leave them all
To go with my love Johnny.

Some say he's dark,
But I say he's bonny,
He's the flower of them all,
My handsome, winsome Johnny.

I know where I'm going,
And I know who's going with me.
I know who I love,
But the dear knows who I'll marry.

TRADITIONAL

THE WATER IS WIDE

The water is wide, I cannot get o'er,
And neither have I wings to fly,
Give me a boat that will carry two,
And both shall row, my love and I.

Down in the meadows the other day,
A-gathering flowers both fine and gay,
A-gathering flowers both red and blue
I little thought what love can do.

I leaned my back up against some oak,
Thinking that he was a trusty tree,
But first he bended and then he broke
And so did my false love to me.

I put my hand into the bush,
Thinking the fairest flower to find.

I pricked my finger to the bone,
But oh, I left the rose behind.

A ship there is and she sails the sea,
She's loaded deep as deep can be;
But not so deep as the love I'm in,
I know not if I sink or swim.

Love is handsome and love is kind,
And love's a jewel when she is new.
But when it is old, it groweth old
And fades away like the morning dew.

TRADITIONAL

A RED, RED ROSE

O my Luve's like a red, red rose,
  That's newly sprung in June.
O my Luve's like the melodie
  That'sweetly play'd in tune.

As fair art thou, my bonie lass,
  So deep in luve am I;
And I will love thee still, my Dear,
  Till a' the seas gang dry.

Till a' the seas gang dry, my Dear,
And the rocks melt wi' the sun:
I will love thee still, my Dear,
While the sands o' life shall run;

And fare thee weel, my only Luve!
And fare thee weel, a while!
And I will come again, my Luve,
Tho' it ware ten thousand mile!

ROBERT BURNS

THE FINDING OF MOSES

On Egypt's banks, contagious to the Nile,
The ould Pharoah's daughter, she went to bathe in style.
She took her dip and came unto the land,
And to dry her royal pelt she ran along the strand.
A bull-rush tripped her where upon she saw
A smiling baby in a wad of straw;
She took him up and says she in accents mild
'Oh tearanages, girls, now, which of yis owns the child?'

She took him up and she gave a little grin,

For she and Moses were standing in their skin.
'Bedad, now,' says she, 'it was someone very rude
Left the little baby by the river in his nude.'
She took him to her ould lad sitting on the throne
'Da,' says she, 'will you give the boy a home?'
'Bedad, now,' says he, 'sure I've often brought in
worse.
Go my darlin' daughter and get the child a nurse.'

Well they sent a bellman to the market square,
To see if he could find a slavey there.
But the only one that he could find
Was the little young one that left the child behind.
She came up to Pharoah, a stranger, mar dhea,
Never lettin' on that she was the baby's ma.
And so little Moses got his mammy back,
Shows that coincidence is a nut to crack.

ZOZIMUS [MICHAEL MORAN]

THEREBY HANGS A TALE

THE WHITE BEAR AND THE ARCTIC FOX

A white bear and an arctic fox
hid in a cave in the snow.
Men with guns were out there.
  They wished they'd go.

Bear looked at fox and said
'I wish we weren't white.
That's why they want us.
  We shine at night.'

Fox sneered and shook his tail.
'We're not in the sky.'
Then he stopped and said
  'Tell me why.'

Bear asked 'Are you crazy?
We can't get away.
This is our habitat.
  We can't fly.'

'We can't sit and wait here'
said the irate fox.
'Soon they'll be building
  apartment blocks

with ice, in Arctic City,
and we'll be the rugs.
If we don't do something
  we're dead mugs.

We can't go south, OK?
We need it white.
Where's whiter than the ball
  that shines at night?'

'But how do we get up there?'
asked the startled bear.
'And if we managed it
  would we have air?'

As they argued like this
the hunters found them
and before they could run
  they shot them.

MATTHEW SWEENEY

HENRY, MY SON

'Oh where have ye been all day, Henry, my son?
O where have ye been all day, my beloved one?'
'Away on the meadow, away on the meadow,
Make my bed I've a pain in my head and I want to lie
  down.'

'And what did you have to eat, Henry, my son?
What did you have to eat, my beloved one?'

'Poison beans, poison beans.'

'And what will you leave your mother, Henry, my son?
What will you leave your mother, my beloved one?'
'A wooling vest, a wooling vest.'

'And what will you leave your brother, Henry, my son?
What will you leave your brother, my beloved one?'
'A blue suit, a blue suit.'

'And what will you leave your father, Henry, my son?
What will you leave your father, my beloved one?'
'A watch and a chain, a watch and a chain.'

'And what will you leave your children, Henry, my son?
What will you leave your children, my beloved one?'
'The sun and the moon, the sun and the moon.'

'And what will you leave your sweetheart, Henry, my son
What will you leave your sweetheart, my beloved one?'
'A rope to hang her, a rope to hang her.'

TRADITIONAL

Frankie and Johnny

Frankie and Johnny were lovers,
Lordy, how they could love,
Swore to be true to each other,
True as the stars above,
He was her man, but he done her wrong.

Little Frankie was a good gal,
As everybody knows,
She did all the work around the house,
And pressed her Johnny's clothes,
He was her man but he done her wrong.

Johnny was a yeller man,
With coal black, curly hair,
Everyone up in St Louis
Thought he was a millionaire,
He was her man, but he done her wrong.

Frankie went down to the bar-room,
Called for a bottle of beer,
Says, 'Looky here, Mister Bartender,
Has my lovin' Johnny been here?
He is my man, and he's doin' me wrong.'

'I will not tell you no story,
I will not tell you no lie.
Johnny left here about an hour ago,
With a gal named Nelly Bly,
He is your man and he's doing you wrong.'

Little Frankie went down Broadway,
With her pistol in her hand,
Said, 'Stand aside you chorus gals,
I'm lookin' for my man,
He is my man, and he's doin' me wrong.'

The first time she shot him, he staggered,
The next time she shot him, he fell,
The last time she shot, O Lawdy,
There was a new man's face in hell,
She shot her man, for doin' her wrong.

'Turn me over doctor,
Turn me over slow,
I got a bullet in my left hand side,
Great God, it's hurtin' me so.
I was her man, but I done her wrong.'

It was a rubber-tyred buggy,
Decorated hack,
Took poor Johnny to the graveyard,
Brought little Frankie back,
He was her man, but he done her wrong.

It was not murder in the first degree,
It was not murder in the third,
A woman simply dropped her man
Like a hunter drops his bird,
She shot her man, for doin' her wrong.

The last time I saw Frankie,

She was sittin' in the 'lectric chair,
Waitin' to go and meet her God
With the sweat runnin' out of her hair.
She shot her man, for doin' her wrong.

Walked on down Broadway
As far as I could see,
All I could hear was a two string bow
Playin' 'Nearer my God to thee'.
He was her man, and he done her wrong.

TRADITIONAL

THE OUTLAW OF LOCH LENE

O many a day have I made good ale in the glen,
That came not of stream or malt, like the brewing of men:
My bed was the ground; my roof, the green-wood above;
And the wealth that I sought, one far kind glance from my Love.

Alas, on the night when the horses I drove from the field
That I was not near from terror my angel to shield!
She stretched forth her arms; her mantle she flung to the wind,
And swam o'er Loch Lene, her outlawed lover to find.

O would that a freezing sleet-winged tempest did sweep,
And I and my love were alone, far off on the deep;
I'd ask not a ship, or a bark, or a pinnace, to save –
With her hand round my waist, I'd fear not the wind or
the wave.

'Tis down by the lake where the wild tree fringes its sides,
The maid of my heart, my fair one of Heaven resides:
I think, as at eve she wanders its mazes among,
The birds go to sleep by the sweet wild twist of her song.

JEREMIAH JOHN CALLANAN

BALLAD OF THE BREAD MAN

Mary stood in the kitchen
Baking a loaf of bread.
An angel flew in through the window.
'We've a job for you,' he said.

'God in his big gold heaven,
Sitting in his big blue chair,
Wanted a mother for his little son.
Suddenly saw you there.'

Mary shook and trembled,

'It isn't true what you say.'
'Don't say that,' said the angel.
'The baby's on its way.'

Joseph was in the workshop
Planing a piece of wood.
'The old man's past it,' the neighbours said.
'That girl's been up to no good.'

'And who was that elegant fellow,'
They said, 'in the shiny gear?'
The things they said about Gabriel
Were hardly fit to hear.

Mary never answered,
Mary never replied.
She kept the information,
Like the baby, safe inside.

It was election winter.
They went to vote in town.
When Mary found her time had come
The hotels let her down.

The baby was born in an annexe
Next to the local pub.
At midnight, a delegation
Turned up from the Farmers' Club.

They talked about an explosion
That made a hole in the sky,

Said they'd been sent to the Lamb and Flag
To see God come down from on high.

A few days later a bishop
And a five-star general were seen
With the head of an African country
In a bullet-proof limousine.

'We've come,' they said, 'with tokens
For the little boy to choose.'
Told the tale abut war and peace
In the television news.

After them came the soldiers
With rifle and bomb and gun,
Looking for enemies of the state.
The family had packed and gone.

When they got back to the village
The neighbours said, to a man,
'That boy will never be one of us,
Though he does what he blessed well can.'

He went round to all the people
A paper crown on his head.
Here is some bread from my father.
Take, eat, he said.

Nobody seemed very hungry.
Nobody seemed to care.
Nobody saw the god in himself

Quietly standing there.

He finished up in the papers,
He came to a very bad end.
He was charged with bringing the living to life.
No man was that prisoner's friend.

There's only one kind of punishment
To fit that kind of a crime.
They rigged a trial and shot him dead.
They were only just in time.

They lifted the young man by the leg,
They lifted him by the arm,
They locked him in a cathedral
In case he came to harm.

They stored him safe as water
Under seven rocks.
One Sunday morning he burst out
Like a jack-in-the-box.

Through the town he went walking.
He showed them the holes in his head.
Now do you want any loaves? he cried.
'No today,' they said.

CHARLES CAUSLEY

The Nose
(after Gogol)

The nose went away by itself
in the early morning
while its owner was asleep.
It walked along the road
sniffing at everything.

It thought: I have a personality of my own.
Why should I be attached to a body?
I haven't been allowed to flower.
So much of me has been wasted.

And it felt wholly free.
It almost began to dance
The world was so full of scents
it had had no time to notice,

when it was attached to a face
weeping, being blown,
catching all sorts of germs
and changing colour.

But now it was quite at ease
bowling merrily along
like a hoop or a wheel,
a factory packed with scent.

And all would have been well
but that, round about evening,

having no eyes for guides,
it staggered into the path
of a mouth, and it was gobbled
rapidly like a sausage
and chewed by great sour teeth –
and that was how it died.

IAN CRICHTON SMITH

Gifts
from
the
Past

A NARROW FELLOW IN THE GRASS

A narrow fellow in the grass
Occasionally rides;
You may have met him – did you not?
His notice sudden is.

The grass divides as with a comb
A spotted shaft is seen
And then it closes at your feet
And opens further on.

He likes a boggy acre,
A floor too cool for corn.
Yet when a child, and barefoot,
I more than once, at morn,

Have passed, I thought, a whip-lash
Upbraiding in the sun –
When, stooping to secure it,
It wrinkled, and was gone.

Several of nature's people
I know, and they know me;
I feel for them a transport
Of cordiality;

But never met this fellow,
Attended or alone,
Without a tighter breathing,
And zero at the bone.

EMILY DICKINSON

The Splendour Falls

The splendour falls on castle walls
  and snowy summits old in story:
The long light shakes across the lakes,
  And the wild cataract leaps in glory,
Blow, bugle, blow, set the wild echoes flying,
Blow, bugle; answer, echoes, dying, dying, dying.

  O hark, O hear! how thin and clear,
    And thinner, clearer, farther going!
  O sweet and far from cliff and scar
  The horns of Elfland faintly blowing!
Blow, let us hear the purple glens replying:
Blow, bugle; answer, echoes, dying, dying, dying.

  O love, they die in yon rich sky,
    They faint on hill or field or river:
  Our echoes roll from soul to soul,
    And grow for ever and for ever.
Blow, bugle, blow, set the wild echoes flying,
And answer, echoes, answer, dying, dying, dying.

LORD TENNYSON

Winter

When icicles hang by the wall,
  And Dick the shepherd blows his nail,
And Tom bears logs into the hall,
  And milk comes frozen home in pail;
When blood is nipped, and ways be foul,
Then nightly sings the staring owl.
Tu-whit, tu-who! a merry note,
While greasy Joan doth keel the pot.

When all aloud the wind doth blow,
  And coughing drowns the parson's saw,
And birds sit brooding in the snow,
  And Marian's nose looks red and raw,
When roasted crabs hiss in the bowl,
Then nightly sings the staring owl,
Tu-whit, to-who! a merry note,
While greasy Joan doth keel the pot.

William Shakespeare

THE TYGER

Tyger! Tyger! burning bright
In the forests of the night,
What immortal hand or eye
Could frame thy fearful symmetry?

In what distant deeps or skies
Burnt the fire of thine eyes?
On what wings dare he aspire?
What the hand dare seize the fire?

And what shoulder, and what art,
Could twist the sinews of thy heart?
And when thy heart began to beat,
What dread hand? and what dread feet?

What the hammer? what the chain?
In what furnace was thy brain?
What the anvil? what dread grasp
Dare its deadly terrors clasp?

When the stars threw down their spears,
And water'd heaven with their tears,
Did he smile his work to see?
Did he who made the Lamb make thee?

Tyger! Tyger! burning bright
In the forests of the night,
What immortal hand or eye
Dare frame thy fearful symmetry?

WILLIAM BLAKE

The Song of Wandering Aengus

I went out to the hazel wood,
Because a fire was in my head,
And cut and peeled a hazel wand,
And hooked a berry to a thread;
And when white moths were on the wing,
And moth-like stars were flickering out,
I dropped the berry in a stream
And caught a little silver trout.

When I had laid it on the floor
I went to blow the fire aflame,
But something rustled on the floor,
And some one called me by my name:
It had become a glimmering girl
With apple blossom in her hair
Who called me by my name and ran
And faded through the brightening air.

Though I am old with wandering
Through hollow lands and hilly lands,
I will find out where she has gone,
And kiss her lips and take her hands;
And walk among long dappled grass,
And pluck till time and times are done
The silver apples of the moon,
The golden apples of the sun.

W. B. Yeats

IN TIME OF 'THE BREAKING OF NATIONS'

Only a man harrowing clods
  In a slow silent walk
With an old horse that stumbles and nods
  Half asleep as they stalk.

Only thin smoke without flame
  From the heaps of couch-grass;
Yet this will go onward the same
  Though Dynasties pass.

Yonder a maid and her wight
  Come whispering by:
War's annals will cloud into night
  Ere their story die.

THOMAS HARDY

ELEGY ON THE DEATH OF A MAD DOG

Good people all, of every sort,
  Give ear unto my song;
And if you find it wondrous short,
  It cannot hold you long.

In Islington there was a man,
  Of whom the world might say,
That still a godly race he ran,
  Whene'er he went to pray.

A kind and gentle heart he had,
  To comfort friends and foes;
The naked every day he clad,
  When he put on his clothes.

And in that town a dog was found,
  As many dogs there be,
Both mongrel, puppy, whelp, and hound,
  And curs of low degree.

This dog and man at first were friends;
  But when a pique began,
The dog, to gain some private ends,
  Went mad and bit the man.

Around from all the neighbouring streets
  The wondering neighbours ran,
And swore the dog had lost his wits,
  To bite so good a man.

The wound it seem'd both sore and sad
  To every Christian eye;
And while they swore the dog was mad,
  They swore the man would die.

But soon a wonder came to light,

That show'd the rogues they lied:
The man recover'd of the bite,
The dog it was that died.

OLIVER GOLDSMITH

THE ANCIENT MARINER *(extract)*

The fair breeze blew, the white foam flew,
The furrow followed free;
We were the first that ever burst
Into that silent sea.

Down dropt the breeze, the sails dropt down,
'Twas sad as sad could be;
And we did speak only to break
The silence of the sea!

All in a hot and copper sky,
The bloody Sun, at noon,
Right up above the mast did stand,
No bigger than the Moon.

Day after day, day after day,
We stuck, nor breath nor motion;
As idle as a painted ship

Upon a painted ocean.

Water, water, every where,
And all the boards did shrink;
Water, water, every where,
Nor any drop to drink.

SAMUEL TAYLOR COLERIDGE

MOMENTS

Broken Day

I don't care
how high the clouds are,
how white they curdle
in the whey of the sky,
or if the sun
is kind to the flowers,
or why the wind
plays at storms in the trees:

the robin hiding
in the garden bushes
has a broken wing

Raymond Souster

The Strand

The dotted line my father's ashplant made
On Sandymount Strand
Is something else the tide won't wash away.

Seamus Heaney

The Errand

'On you go now! Run, son, like the devil
And tell your mother to try
To find me a bubble for the spirit level
And a new knot for this tie.'

But still he was glad, I know, when I stood my ground,
Putting it up to him
With a smile that trumped his smile and his fool's
errand,
Waiting for the next move in the game.

Seamus Heaney

At Nine of the Night I Opened My Door

At nine of the night I opened my door
That stands midway between moor and moor,
And all around me, silver-bright,
I saw that the world had turned to white.

Thick was the snow on field and hedge
And vanished was the river-sedge,
Where winter skilfully had wound
A shining scarf without a sound.

And as I stood and gazed my fill
A stable-boy came down the hill.
With every step I saw him take
Flew at his heel a puff of flake.

His brow was whiter than the hoar,
A beard of freshest snow he wore,
And round about him, snow-flake starred,
A red horse-blanket from the yard.

In a red cloak I saw him go,
His back was bent, his step was slow,
And as he laboured through the cold
He seemed a hundred winters old.

I stood and watched the snowy head,
The whiskers white, the cloak of red.
'A Merry Christmas!' I heard him cry.
'The same to you, old friend,' said I.

CHARLES CAUSLEY

Night Herons

It was after a day's rain:
the street facing the west
was lit with growing yellow;
the black road gleamed.

First one child looked and saw
and told another.
Face after face, the windows
flowered with eyes.

It was like a long fuse lighted,
the news travelling.
No one called out loudly;
everyone said 'Hush.'

The light deepened; the wet road
answered in daffodil colours,
and down its centre
walked the two tall herons.

Stranger than wild birds, even,
what happened on those faces:
suddenly believing in something,
they smiled and opened.

Children thought of fountains,
circuses, swans feeding:
women remembered words
spoken when they were young.

Everyone said 'Hush;'
no one spoke loudly;
but suddenly the herons
rose and were gone. The light faded.

JUDITH WRIGHT

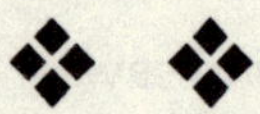

SWANS IN THE NIGHT

Three swans
Under the moon,
Three shadows
On the lagoon.

Three swans
On the water ride,
Three shadows
Move beside.

Silver water,
Silent swans,
Swaying ferns
With silvered fronds.

A strolling cloud
Obscures the moon,

Gone the swans
From the dark lagoon.

JOAN MELLINGS

FAIRY STORY

I went into the wood one day
And there I walked and lost my way

When it was so dark I could not see
A little creature came to me

He said if I would sing a song
The time would not be very long

But first I must let him hold my hand tight
Or else the wood would give me a fright

I sang a song, he let me go
But now I am home again there is nobody I know.

STEVIE SMITH

Fog

The fog comes
on little cat feet.

It sits looking
over harbour and city
on silent haunches
and then moves on.

CARL SANDBURG

YOUNG VOICES

The Star

Once upon a night of stars
One saw a little girl looking up at it.
'Don't look at me so hard, little girl.
How I wonder what you are, too.'

Dorothy Jones

Hideout

I live beside a
Field of ideas.

I made a poem hut there
Out of words and branches and things.

There are cows wandering
In my field of ideas.

Cows knock
My poem hut down.

They think my field of ideas
Is their's to eat.

Cows don't understand my poetry.

RUTH HOEY [8]
KILSARAN NS, CO. LOUTH

THE MAGICAL WHITE HORSE

I saw a horse one diamond sky night,
When all the stars were shining bright.
It galloped wildly through the sky.
Did anyone else see it other than I?

It had glittering eyes and long white ears,
It jumped the fence and disappeared,
It vanished in a puff of smoke,
But when I tell Mam, she thinks it's a joke.

I know I saw it in the sky.
But did anyone see it other than I?

NICOLA SHERRY [9]
SCOIL PHÁDRAIG, CORRACRIN, EMYVALE,
CO. MONAGHAN

Norman the Conqueror

Envied by all pupils is Norman
Who dared to brave the trap-door
Down
Down
Down
Below the stage.

What did he find there?
Confiscated comics?
A secret laboratory?
Or a porthole to another dimension?

Norman likes to keep them guessing ...

David Shaw
Seaview PS, Belfast

I Wonder Why?

I wonder why flower stem is green, sky so blue,
air never seen.
I wonder why the bees begin to hum,
Just before the spring days are done.
I wonder why turtles are slow, hares fast,
and lions stoop so very low.

I wonder why Santa's red, why not green,
why not purple instead.
I wonder why tooth fairies fly,
Why are we on ground instead of in sky.
These answers I shall never know, although
I wonder so and so.
Why man made first, why not woman,
These answers I shall never know.

ELAINE O'RIORDAN [10]
SCOIL BHARRA, INISHMORE, BALLINCOLLIG, CO. CORK

SHINING THINGS

I love all shining things,
I love gleaming purple butterfly wings
That sail across the sky in spring,
And that's why I love shining things.

I like the way my doorbell glows
And the golden button on my teddy bear's nose.
I like blue feathers on swallows' wings
And they are some of my shining things.

The paper in my classroom glows and shines
And the glistening dewdrops in this garden of mine.
The woman that lives down the street

Wears shining slippers on her feet.

And the old man that lives down the road,
His eyes go shiny when he lifts his load.
You see shining things are special to me
And to you and to all the world too.

DAMIEN MOONEY [9]
ST LORCAN'S BNS, PALMERSTOWN, DUBLIN

LISTEN

Listen to the beat
Of the feet,
Listen to the tube trains
Down underneath.

Listen to the sea crash
Around,
Listen to the children
In the playground.

Listen to the bus
Stop and go,
Listen to the squirrel
Run to and fro.

Listen to the screech
Of the women,
Listen to the splash
Of someone swimming.

Isn't it just great sitting there,
Listening to all the things that are everywhere.

JAMES O'SULLIVAN [11]
SCOIL MHUIRE NA TRÓCAIRE, BUTTEVANT, CO. CORK

AVRIL

I came home from school on that
Warm summer's day.
I walked down the rough stony lane.
My father sood outside peering helplessly
At the window.
My mother ran out the brown door
Tears ran down her pale cheeks as
She walked me to our neighbour's house.
Neil and Eimear were there
Confused like me.
We played quietly with Lego.
That evening we were left home.
Relations and friends were there sitting around
the blazing fire talking quietly to each other.

They sipped cups of tea all saying how sorry they were.
But there was no cuddly baby in the cot.

GAVIN DALY, ST KILLIAN'S NS
CROSSREAGH, MULLAGH, CO. CAVAN

AUTUMN INSIDE

Being wrapped up
in my warm woolly quilt
looking out the window
The wet and windy breeze
makes me feel nice and cosy
and when the rain
lashes against the glass
It is my friend.

CHRISTOPHER LYNCH, ST KILLIAN'S NS
CROSSREAGH, MULLAGH, CO. CAVAN

THE LOCKED DOOR (I)

I can see you
Playing among yourselves
But not with me.

I can see you
Passing notes around the class
But none ever come to me.

I can hear you
Shouting and laughing
But not with me.

I can hear you
Planning an outing to the town
But you don't invite me.

I plead with you
But never will you let me in.

BEN GREEN, DALKEY PROJECT NS
GLENAGEARY, CO. DUBLIN

Death of a Calf

Opening the door, I
switched the light on.
His mother lowed
angrily at me.

There he lay,
eyes shut,
His body cosy
in the straw.

'A weak one, he'll
not last long.'
My father studied the
calf's delicate features.

Suddenly he moved,
opened his eyes.
Kicked his legs and then ....
He was gone.

Noelle O'Brien, St Killian's NS
Crossreagh, Mullagh, Co. Cavan

Wet Fields

As I was walking out the gap,
I heard the loud voice of my father,
'Get the cows', he shouted,
As I was walking up the field
I could hear the water
Under my wellington,
Splashing out each side.

When I reached the gap
At the top of the field,
There the cows were,
Under a tree,
Sheltering from the rain,
It was getting heavier
At this time I
hated the fields.

Shane Osborne, St Killian's NS
Crossreagh, Mullagh, Co. Cavan

Nobody Knows

Deep in the forest
Behind the waterfall
There lies a place nobody knows
Where the water bounces
on the rocks
on its journey to the sea
and on hot summer days
I stand underneath
and feel the cool water
Rush under my feet
It's here I feel at home
It's here I feel safe
It's here that there is my
Secret Place.

Eilish McCabe, St Killian's NS
Crossreagh, Mullagh, Co. Cavan

Gran's Dresser

It stood in Gran's kitchen
Showing off all her delph,
Cups, bowls, and plates
Filled every shelf.

Even when I can't see it
It's there in my mind ....
– The good-sides faced outwards
And the cracks turned behind.

Each item displayed
Was a very great treasure,
Not for its worth
But just for its pleasure.

For the dresser was a book
And the delph its pages,
That carried Gran's story
Down through the ages –

A story of life,
Its joy and its sorrow
The hopes of today
And the fears of tomorrow.

KERRY RUSSELL, MOYLE NS
NEWTOWNCUNNINGHAM, CO. DONEGAL

My Grandad

I never met my grandad
He died when I was two,
He was 66 when he died
And his eyes were greenie-blue.

His hobbies were driving and gardening
He loved eating tomatoes and ham (but not together)
He was very proud of his grandchildren
And was a very witty man.

He used to call me Jennifer Jones
My Mum just doesn't know why,
Then again there's a lot she doesn't know
Like why did he have to die?

Jennifer McAndrew [10]
St Patrick's Loreto NS, Bray

Lullaby of the Mountains

Rat do not squeak,
Bug do not creep
While the night spreads
Over the mountain.

Wind do not whistle,
Do not prick thistle
While the animals
Sleep on the mountain.

FIONA BUSHE [11]
ST PATRICK'S LORETO NS, BRAY

Words at Play

Conundrums

Tell me a word
that you've often heard,
yet it makes you squint
if you see it in print!

Tell me a thing
that you've often seen,
yet if put in a book
it makes you turn green!

Tell me a thing
that you often do,
which described in a story
shocks you through and through!

Tell me what's wrong
with words or with you
that you don't mind the thing
yet the name is taboo.

D. H. Lawrence

Blum

Dog means dog,
And cat means cat;
And there are lots
Of words like that.

A cart's a cart
To pull or shove,
A plate's a plate
To eat off of.

But there are other
Words I say
When I am left
Alone to play.

Blum is one.
Blum is a word
That very few
Have ever heard.

I like to say it,
'Blum, Blum, Blum' –
I do it loud
Or in a hum.

All by itself
It's nice to sing:
It does not mean
A single thing.

Dorothy Aldis

My Uncle Robert

My Uncle Robert
is bald as a coot,
and he polishes his skull
just like a boot.
On a hot day his head
reflects the sun's heat,
burning the soles
of flying birds' feet.

Michael Dugan

Marvels

The man in the wilderness said to me,
How many strawberries grow in the sea?
I answered him as I thought good,
As many red herrings as grow in the wood.

Anon.

ENDLESS CHANT

'Who put the overalls in Mrs Murphy's chowder?'
Nobody answered, so she said it all the louder:
'Who put the overalls in Mrs Murphy's chowder?'
Nobody answered, so she said it all the louder:
'Who put the overalls in Mrs Murphy's chowder?'
Nobody answered, so she said it all the louder:
'Who put the overalls in Mrs Murphy's chowder?'
Nobody answered, so she said it all the louder:
'Who put the overalls in Mrs Murphy's chowder?'
Nobody answered, so she said it all the louder:
'Who put the overalls in Mrs Murphy's chowder?'
Nobody answered, so she said it all the louder:
'Who put the overalls in Mrs Murphy's chowder?'
Nobody answered, so she said it all the louder:
'Who put the overalls in Mrs Murphy's chowder?'
Nobody answered, so she said it all the louder:
'Who put the overalls in Mrs Murphy's chowder?'
Nobody answered, so she said it all the louder:
'Who put the overalls in Mrs Murphy's chowder?'
Nobody answered, so she said it all the louder:
'Who put the overalls in Mrs Murphy's chowder?'
Nobody answered, so she said it all the louder:
'Who put the overalls in Mrs Murphy's chowder?'
Nobody answered, so she said it all the louder:
'Who put the overalls in Mrs Murphy's chowder?'
Nobody answered, so she said it all the louder:
'Who put the overalls in Mrs Murphy's chowder?'

Nobody answered, so she said it all the louder:
'Who put the overalls in Mrs Murphy's chowder?'
Nobody answered, so she said it all the louder:
'Who put the overalls in Mrs Murphy's chowder?'
Nobody answered, so she said it all the louder:
'Who put the overalls in Mrs Murphy's chowder?'
Nobody answered, so she said it all the louder:
'Who put the overalls in Mrs Murphy's chowder?'
Nobody answered, so she said it all the louder:
'Who put the overalls in Mrs Murphy's chowder?'
Nobody answered, so she said it all the louder:
'Who put the overalls in Mrs Murphy's chowder?'
Nobody answered, so she said it all the louder:
'Who put the overalls in Mrs Murphy's chowder?'

TRADITIONAL

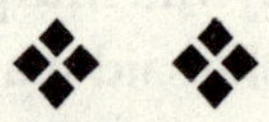

Parodies of MARY HAD A LITTLE LAMB

Mary had a little lamb,
Its feet were black as soot,
And into Mary's bread and jam
Its sooty foot it put.

Now Mary was a careful child,
Avoided every sham,
She said – one little word that meant
The mother of that lamb.

Mary had a little lamb,
It was a greedy glutton.
She fed it on ice-cream all day
And now it's frozen mutton.

Mary had a little cow,
It fed on safety pins:
And every time she milked the cow
The milk came out in tins.

Mary had a little lamb,
She also had a bear;
I've often seen her little lamb,
But I've never seen her *bear*

ANON

Order in the court

Order in the court
The judge is eating beans
His wife is in the bath tub
Shooting submarines.

Traditional

Through the teeth

Through the teeth
And past the gums
Look out stomach,
Here it comes!

Traditional

The Cats of Kilkenny

There were once two cats of Kilkenny,
Each thought there was one cat too many,
So they fought and they fit,
And they scratched and they bit,
Till, excepting their nails
And the tips of their tails,
Instead of two cats, there weren't any.

Anon.

Way Down South

Way down South where bananas grow,
A grasshopper stepped on an elephant's toe.
The elephant said, with tears in his eyes,
'Pick on somebody your own size.'

Anon.

'Charlie'

Mooses come from Moos-issippi
Cats from Katmandu
Rhinos come from the River Rhine
And kittens from Purr-oo
Parrots come from Polly-nesia
(So the story goes)
But where our puppy Charlie comes from
Goodness only knows!

Rabbits come from Bunny Scotland
(Where they breed in hordes)
Beetles come from Liverpool
And crickets come from Lords.
Elephants come from Tuscaloosa
Bucks from Timbuctoo
But where our puppy Charlie comes from
Haven't got a clue!

Honeybears hail from Honey-lulu
(As you may have guessed)
Blubber comes from Wales, of course,
And Robins come from Brest.
Otters come from Ottawa
And Pekes from Picardy
But where our puppy Charlie comes from
Don't
ask
me!

Herbert Kretzmer

When I Was Three

When I was three I had a friend
Who asked me why bananas bend,
I told him why, but now I'm four
I'm not so sure ...

Richard Edwards

Have You Ever Seen?

Have you ever seen
a blue tadpole
Have you ever seen
a spoilt-brat toad

Have you ever seen
a walking fish
Have you ever seen
a grunting chick

Have you ever seen
a singing spider
Have you ever seen
a dancing tiger

Have you ever seen

a monkey swimming
Have you ever seen
a turtle grinning

Have you ever?

ANON.

Acknowledgements

The editor and publisher would like to thank the following for permission to reprint material:
David Higham Associates for the following poems by Charles Causley – 'Ballad of the Bread Man', 'Brigid', 'Dream Poem', 'My Mother saw a Dancing Bear', 'Tom Bone', 'Hawthorn White', 'At Nine of Night' and 'Early in the Morning' from *Collected Poems for Children,* Macmillan 1997; The Literary Trustees of Walter de La Mare, and the Society of Authors as their representatives for 'The Window' and 'Someone', *The Complete Poems of Walter de la Mare,* 1969 (USA 1970) and 'In the Orchard' by James Stephens; Sheil Land Associates Ltd for 'The Star' by Dorothy Jones from *Reach Out Book* 2, edited by Blackburn and Cunningham, Routledge & Keegan Paul; James Clarke & Co. Ltd./ The Lutterworth Press for 'The Door' by Richard Edwards, *The Word Party,* 1986; Faber and Faber for 'After the Rains' by N. M. Bodecker from *Snowman Sniffles,* 'Running Lightly' from 'The Last Son' by Theodore Roethke, 'Conundrums' by D. H. Lawrence, *Collected Poems,* 'The Strand' and 'The Errand' by Seamus Heaney, *The Spirit Level,* 1997, 'The White Bear and Artic Fox' by Matthew Sweeney, *The Flying Spring Onions;* Joan Mellings for her 'Swans in the Night'; Myfany Thomas for 'Tall Nettles' and 'Out in the Dark' by Edward Thomas, *Collected Poems,* Oxford University Press; Felicity Bryan for 'Monster' and 'When I was Three' from *The Word Party,* copyright © Richard Edwards 1986; James MacGibbon for Stevie Smith's 'Fairy Story', *The Collected Poems of Stevie Smith* (Penguin 20th Century Classics); A. P. Watt on behalf of Michael Yeats for 'The Song of Wandering Aengus' by W. B. Yeats, *Collected Poems of W. B. Yeats,* 1965; F. Sommerville and the Estate of E. Starkey for 'A Piper' by Seumas O'Sullivan; 'The Lurkers' Copyright © Adrian Henri 1986. Reproduced by permission of the author, c/o Rogers, Coleridge & White Ltd., 20 Powis Mews, London W11 1JN; 'Fog' from *Chicago Poems* by Carl Sandburg, copyright 1916 by Holt, Rinehart and Winston and renewed 1944 by Carl Sandburg, reprinted by permission of Harcourt Brace and Company; Thomas McCarthy for his poem 'Her Blindness'; Herbert Kretzmer for his poem 'Charlie'; 'I'm Nobody! Who are You?' and 'A Narrow Fellow', reprinted by

permission of the publishers and the Trustees of Amherst College from *The Poems of Emily Dickinson*, Thomas H. Johnson, ed., Cambridge, Mass: The Belknap Press of Harvard University Press, Copyright © 1951, 1955, 1979, 1983 by the President and Fellows of Harvard College; Victor Gollancz for 'The Nose' by Ian Crichton Smith from *Love Poems and Elegies;* Blake Morrison for 'Seahorse'; 'Broken Day' is reprinted from *Collected Poems of Raymond Souster* by permission of Oberon Press; 'Blum' by Dorothy Aldis reprinted by permission of G. P. Putnam's Sons from *Here, There and Everywhere,* copyright 1927, 1928, 1955, 1956 by Dorothy Aldis; Harper Collins Publishers for 'Night Herons' by Judith Wright from *Collected* Poems, 'The Pudding Song' by Norman Lindsay from *The Magic Pudding;* Devin-Adair Publishers for 'She Moved through the Fair' by Padraic Colum; Michael Dugan for 'Summer and Winter' and 'My Uncle Robert'; Gerry Sheanon and St Killian's NS for 'Nobody Knows' by Eilish McCabe, 'Autumn Inside' by Christopher Lynch, 'Wet Fields' by Shane Osborne and 'Death of a Calf' by Noelle O'Brien from *A Carpet of Leaves;* Kerry Russell (Moyle NS) for 'Gran's Dresser', Ben Green (Dalkey Project NS) for 'The Locked Door', David Shaw (Seaview PS) for 'Norman', Gavin Daly (St Killian's NS) for 'Avril' from *The Pushkin Prizes* publications; Ruth Hoey (Kilsaran NS) for 'Hideout', Nicola Sherry (Scoil Phádraig) for 'The Magical White Horse', Damien Mooney (St Lorcan's BNS) for 'Shining Things', Elaine O'Riordan (Scoil Barra NS) for 'I Wonder Why', James O'Sullivan (Scoil Mhuire na Trócaire) for 'Listen', Jennifer McAndrew (St Patrick's Loreto NS) for 'My Grandad', Fiona Bushe (St Patrick's Loreto NS) for 'Lullaby of the Mountain' from *Telepoems 1995*

Every effort has been made to trace the owners of copyright material and it is hoped that no copyright has been infringed. If we have inadvertently infringed any copyright we apologise and we would be grateful to be notified of any errors or omissions in the above list and will be happy to make good any such errors or omissions at the first opportunity.

Real Cool
Poems to Grow Up With

Edited by Niall MacMonagle

This upbeat and original collection gathers together works by Irish and international poets of the first rank, guaranteed to appeal to young people and even, perhaps, to throw light on some of the shadows of troubled adolescent years.

The anthology features poems such as 'The Moment' by Sharon Olds, 'Nessa' by Paul Durken, 'Almost Communication' by Rita Ann Higgins, 'Aunt Jennifer's Tigers' by Adrienne Rich, 'Everything is Going to Be All Right' by Derek Mahon, 'Field of Vison' by Seamus Heaney, Carol Ann Duffy's 'In Mrs Tilscher's Class' and other poets including Paula Meehan, Simon Armitage, Fluer Adcock, Mary Oliver, Robert Frost, Wendy Cope, Peter Reading and Brendan Kennelly.

Enchanted Irish Tales

Patricia Lynch

Enchanted Irish Tales tells of ancient heroes and heroines, fantastic deeds of bravery, magical kingdoms, weird and wonderful animals. This illustrated edition of classical folktales, retold by Patricia Lynch with all the imagination and warmth for which she is renowned, rekindles the age-old legends of Ireland, as exciting today as they were when first told. This collection includes: Conary Mór and the Three Red Riders, The Long Life of Tuan MacCarrell, Finn MacCool and the Fianna, Oisín and the Land of Youth, The Kingdom of the Dwarfs, The Dragon Ring of Connla, Mac Datho's Boar and Ethne.

IRISH STORIES FOR CHILDREN

Selected by TOM MULLINS

Reading stories helps us all to see life in different ways. We can leave behind our ordinary everyday life and enter into other worlds; these can be real or imagined; we can have adventures with heroes and heroines, with ghosts and giants, with animals and monsters which leave us wishing and wondering.

The stories in this book, selected by Tom Mullins, are from some of Ireland's finest writers and they will delight and entertain children of all ages.

GOLDEN APPLES
IRISH POEMS FOR CHILDREN

Edited by JO O'DONOGHUE

Here is a magical new collection of Irish poems for children featuring cats, dogs, squirrels, sheep and lambs – and of course leprechauns and fairies. There are stirring ballads and interesting grown-ups like the Dublin Piper. Great poets like Yeats, Kavanagh, MacNeice and Heaney are included, but also the anonymous versifiers who gave us such gems as 'Brian O'Linn'.

Golden Apples is a collection to treasure.